A Luau at Home

Luaus are a time-honored tradition in Hawaii and are the main function for weddings, graduations, birthday parties, any event where people gather to celebrate. The dishes vary from family to family, but the pork and poi are always available.

In this set of recipes, we have created a luau with ingredients readily available throughout the world.

Simply set your "table" on the floor or grass, with the food and flowers in the center and dig in. Candles and tiki torches set off the mood and fresh flowers are the decoration you need.

A little soft Hawaiian music in the background, guests dressed in bright clothing and a hula contest and you are back in Hawaii.

KALUA PORK

The pig is always the guest of honor at a luau, but that isn't always possible at home. A nice, juicy pork roast will work just as well. Use a boneless roast so you know it will be all meat and, cooked long and slow, it will taste almost like it came out of an imu.

Boneless port roast
Liquid Smoke
2-3 large cloves garlic, minced
1 tablespoon soy sauce
1/2 teaspoon chilli powder

4 tablespoons butter
3 tablespoons rum
2 tablespoons brown sugar
1/2 small jar strained peaches (baby food)
3 oz chopped macadamia nuts

Preheat oven to 500°. Brush roast with Liquid Smoke and garlic; sear in oven for 10 minutes. Reduce heat to 275°. Combine soy sauce and chilli powder. Brush on roast, insert meat thermometer and roast until medium well. Combine butter, rum, brown sugar and peaches in a small saucepan and stir constantly until melted. Brush over roast and sprinkle with nuts. Continue cooking 10-15 minutes. Slice and serve.

Mock Lobster

I have no idea where this recipe originated, but it's been a favorite for more than 15 years. It works great for a luau when you have the grill filled up with chicken and ribs. With all the other food, figure about 6 oz per person.

Solid white fish (red snapper)
1/2 minced onion
1 bay leaf
dash cayenne pepper
dash salt
1 bottle dry white wine

Heat the wine in a heavy skillet until simmering. Add onion, bay leaf, cayenne and salt. Boil pieces of fish 3 to 4 minutes until firm. Drain and serve with melted butter for dipping.

Soy Teriyaki Chicken

Soy Teriyaki Chicken is a favorite in the islands for luaus and family picnics. Marinate the chicken as long as possible, turning often.

3-4 lbs chicken pieces
1 cup soy sauce
1 cup dry white wine
3 tablespoons sugar
2 teaspoons grated ginger root
OR 1 teaspoon powdered ginger
3 cloves garlic, minced
1 teaspoon chilli powder
1 teaspoon Kitchen Bouquet

Combine all ingredients, except chicken, in a large bowl. Add chicken and coat all surfaces. Cover and marinate overnight, turning often. Barbecue over medium coals, basting with marinade, until tender. This also works well cooked over an indoor grill or oven broiled.

Steamed and Fried Rice

Rice is a staple in Hawaii, both white and flavored. The recipe below is for fried rice, but both may be served. When making white rice, be sure to use the long-cooking rice rather than instant because it has a more neutral flavor.

2 cups, uncooked long-grain rice
water
salt

1/4 lb bacon, diced
2 eggs
1/2 lb cooked pork, finely diced
1/4 lb cooked chicken, finely diced
1/2 lb imitation shrimp, or fresh, cooked, finely diced
4 green scallions, thinly sliced
1 teaspoon grated ginger root
dash pepper
3-4 tablespoons soy sauce

Cook rice according to directions on package; drain. Fry bacon in wok or heavy skillet until crisp; set aside. Drain all but 1 tablespoon oil from skillet. Beat eggs and pepper. Pour half of egg mixture into pan and tilt so eggs cover the bottom. Cook until set; remove. Roll and slice into thin strips. Repeat with rest of eggs. Stir fry pork, chicken, shrimp, scallions and ginger until warm; stir in rice and soy sauce. Cook and stir until hot.

Luau Sweet Potatoes

1 large can yams
2 bananas, sliced
1 can (6 1/2 oz) crushed pineapple, or fresh
3 oz chopped macadamia nuts
2 tablespoons rum
1/2 cup brown sugar, packed
4 tablespoons butter, melted

Place yams in an oven-proof dish; add bananas. Combine pineapple, butter, brown sugar and rum and pour over potatoes and bananas. Sprinkle with macadamia nuts. Bake at 350° for 25-30 minutes, until bubbling.

Tropical Fruit Boat

A luau isn't a luau without lots of fresh fruit. Here we've used a combination of exotic fruits with ones common throughout the country. Be sure to vary the colors for pleasing eye appeal. The amount of fruit will depend on the size of your crowd, but figure six people to a half boat shown here.

1 fresh, ripe pineapple
2-3 kiwi fruit
1 box strawberries
2 bananas

Cut pineapple in half and cut out fruit in chunks, leaving the skin intact. Slice the rest of the fruit (brush the bananas with lemon juice) and arrange in hollowed-out pineapples. Garnish with fresh flowers.

Paradise Cake

1 cup vegetable shortening
2 cups sugar
4 eggs, beaten
3 bananas, mashed (by hand, not in a processor)
1 ripe mango or papaya, peeled, seeded and mashed
2 teaspoons salt
1 teaspoon baking soda
3 teaspoons baking powder
6 tablespoons sour milk or cream
2 tablespoons lemon juice
2 cups chopped macadamia nuts
4 cups flour
Grated lemon rind from 1 lemon

Cream shortening and sugar. Add beaten eggs, bananas and mango or papaya. Sift salt, soda, baking powder and flour and add to fruit mixture with milk, lemon juice, rind and nuts.

(You may make sour milk by adding 1 tablespoon lemon juice to regular milk and mixing). Mix well and turn into a well greased bundt pan. Bake at 350° for one hour. Cool in pan.

Topping:
1 (8 oz) package Philadelphia Cream Cheese, room temperature
2 cups whipped cream topping (La Creme is best)
1 cup ground macadamia nuts
1 (oz) can unsweetened pineapple juice

Mix cream cheese and whipped cream topping. Add pineapple juice slowly until reaching a light consistency, about half the can. Top cooled cake with mixture and sprinkle with nuts. May be made a day ahead.

Tiki Punch

If you are having a small enough party, delight your guests with their own "pineapple glass". When you hollow-out the pineapple, take care not to cut through the skin. Use the pineapple for other dishes. It's also a great opportunity to experiment with different garnishes. Recipe serves one.

1 pineapple per guest or couple
1 oz Vodka
1/2 oz Galliano
5 oz orange juice
5 oz pineapple juice
Champagne

Combine Vodka, Galliano, and juices in a pitcher. Pour into pineapples, approximately 2/3 from the top. Fill with Champagne and add garnishes.

Popular Tropical Drinks

When visitors come to the Islands, they are amazed at the huge selection of drinks available, each one better than the one before.

There isn't any magic to them and they are just as good at a party or just sitting with friends on a warm summer day.

The ingredients are available throughout the world and a blender isn't necessary if you have a strong shaker arm.

A cool tropical drink in your hand and a warm summer breeze and you'll be right back in the islands.

Hawaiian Sunset

*As beautiful as the real sunsets of Waikiki, Hawaiian Sunset is perfect for
those who like a sweeter drink.*

2 oz dark rum
1/2 oz Amaretto
1/2 oz Galliano
1/2 oz Grenadine
4 oz pineapple juice

Fill glass with ice. Add rum,
Amaretto, Galliano and pineapple
juice (use more juice, if needed, to
fill glass). Float Grenadine on top.
Garnish with fruit or flowers.

Blue Hawaii

The Blue Hawaii takes after the beautiful blue water of Hawaii's beaches.

1 oz light rum
1 oz blue Curacao
1 oz coconut cream
5 oz pineapple juice
Crushed ice

Combine rum, blue Curacao, coconut cream, juice and crushed ice in a blender; mix well. Garnish with flowers.

Hurricane Robert

This drink was invented through a mistake by a bartender and gives a great flavor to the old stand-by screwdriver.

2 oz Vodka
1 oz Galliano
4 oz pineapple juice
4 oz orange juice

Fill 12 oz glass with ice. Add Vodka, Galliano and juices; mix well.

Mai Tai

There is much discussion about the origin of the delightful Mai Tai. Whoever invented it, the Mai Tai has become one of the most popular drinks in the islands.

2 oz light rum
1 oz dark rum
1 oz Triple Sec orange liqueur
1/2 oz Amaretto
1/2 oz lime juice

Crushed ice
Mix the rums, Triple Sec, Amaretto and lime juice in a 7 oz glass. Add crushed ice and garnish.

Strawberry Daiquiri

The daiquiri is very versatile, allowing you to take advantage of all the wonderful fruits of the islands.

2 oz light rum
1/2 oz lime juice
1 oz Creme de Cassis
1 teaspoon superfine sugar
6-8 strawberries, hulled
Crushed ice

Mix rum, lime juice, Creme de Cassis, sugar, strawberries and crushed ice in a blender; mix well. Pour into a large stemmed glass and garnish with a whole strawberry.
For a pineapple daiquiri, substitute Contreau for Creme de Cassis and 4 oz pineapple juice for strawberries.
For a banana daiquiri, substitute banana liqueur and a banana.

Bird of Paradise

The Bird of Paradise is a refreshing drink after a long day and an attractive addition to any party. Just close your eyes and pretend you are in paradise.

2 oz light rum
1/2 oz banana liqueur
1/2 oz Galliano
4 oz Pineapple juice
Crushed ice

Mix rum, banana liqueur, Galliano and pineapple juice in a blender. Add ice and mix well. Garnish with fruit slices.

Macadamia Chi Chi

This drink combines all the best of Hawaii including the flavor of it's wonderful macadamia nuts. But watch out, they sneak up on you! The coconut cream comes in several forms from syrup to powder and all of them work great.

2 oz Vodka
1 oz coconut cream
1 oz macadamia nut liqueur
4 oz pineapple juice
Crushed ice

Fill blender with crushed ice, Vodka, coconut cream and pineapple juice; mix well. Pour in glass and float macadamia nut liqueur on top. Garnish with pineapple or flowers.

Ethnic Foods of Hawaii

Hawaii is truly the melting pot of the world. Its population is made up of people from every culture.

One of the greatest benefits has been the incredible selection of dishes available in the islands. Influences from the cultures of Japan, China and Philippines have been among the strongest.

This selection of recipes gives an idea of the varied foods of the islands. Any combination will make an enjoyable meal or an addition to your favorite menu.

They are all designed for experimentation, so don't be afraid to add your favorite ingredients and enjoy a world of exciting food.

Chicken Vegetable Stir-Fry

Chinese cooking, besides being good for you, makes use of all types of vegetables and is pretty to serve. Vary the vegetables to include your favorites or leave out the chicken and serve the vegetables as a side dish with your favorite meat.

1 (3 lb) chicken (the pieces you prefer)
Broccoli flowers
Red Bell pepper
1 can baby corn
1 large onion, peeled and sliced lengthwise
Chinese peas, fresh (with strings removed) or frozen and thawed
1 pkg bean sprouts or canned
1/2 lb mushrooms, sliced
3 large garlic cloves, sliced
2-3 teaspoons chicken boullion
1/4 cup soy sauce or to taste
1/2 cup dry sherry
Vegetable oil

Skin chicken and cut into bite-sized pieces; set aside. Prepare vegetables making sure they are all very dry. In a wok or heavy frying pan, heat oil until chicken sizzles. Add the garlic and immediately add chicken pieces stirring constantly with a spoon or chopsticks. When chicken is browned, add uncooked vegetables and stir-fry for 2-3 minutes. Add cooked (canned) vegetables and cook 2 minutes more. Add boullion, soy sauce and sherry and cook for 3-4 minutes. Serve immediately.

Lumpia

This appetizer from the Philippines is also known as egg or spring rolls.
These should be served right away while they are crispy.

3 cups vegetable oil
2 lbs chicken pieces, skinned and diced
1/2 lb boneless pork, diced
1 small onion, diced
1 small green cabbage or Chinese cabbage, chopped
1/4 lb bacon, diced
3 large garlic cloves, chopped
1/2 lb bean sprouts, chopped
1/2 cup celery, strings removed and diced
1/4 cup soy sauce
1 teaspoon grated fresh ginger
1/4 lb mushrooms, diced
Egg roll wrappers

In a heavy skillet, brown bacon and set aside. Brown chicken and pork in bacon fat until cooked, adding vegetable oil, if necessary; set aside. Add garlic, onion, cabbage, bean sprouts, celery and soy sauce and cook until onions and cabbage are soft, adding water if cabbage becomes too dry. Add meat and mix thoroughly. Drain completely in a colander. Place about 1/3 cup filling along the center of each wrapper. Fold in the ends, then roll to cover the filling completely. Heat the oil in a wok or heavy skillet and place 2-3 lumpia at a time in the oil, seam down and fry until golden brown. Drain on paper towels.

Korean Short Ribs

Korean Short Ribs are the Korean equivalent of Japan's teriyaki. Where the thin-cut short ribs are not available, substitute spare ribs, they still taste great.

1 cup packed brown sugar
1/4 level tablespoon fresh ginger
4 large garlic cloves, minced
2 cups soy sauce
1/2 cup dry white wine or sherry
2 teaspoons chilli powder
1/2 teaspoon sesame oil (optional)
Sesame seeds (optional)

Combine ingredients in a large bowl. Add ribs making sure all surfaces are covered. Cover bowl and marinade in refrigerator over night or at least 6 hours. Grill over medium coals until tender, or broil in oven. Sprinkle with sesame seeds before serving.

Tempura

As imposing as tempura looks, it is surprisingly easy to prepare. The vegetables listed below are only suggestions. They may be substituted for almost any you prefer - experiment. Chicken, cut into bite-sized pieces, may be used in addition to or in place of the shrimp. Most important is to have everything cut up before heating the oil and to make sure your oil is hot enough.

2 egg yolks
2 cups ice water
2 cups flour
1/4 teaspoon baking soda
Vegetable oil

Medium to large shrimp, peeled with tail on, and deveined
Sweet potatoes, sliced
Large yellow onions, peeled and cut into rings
Chinese pea pods or whole string beans
(frozen and thawed are OK)
Broccoli flowers and peeled stems
Mushrooms, cleaned and left whole

Soy sauce
Hot Chinese mustard

Prepare all the vegetables and meat; set aside making sure they are all very dry to keep oil from spattering. In a medium bowl, beat egg yolks. Add ice water and mix well. Add flour and baking soda all at once and stir lightly with fork or chopsticks just to combine. Heat oil in wok or heavy frying pan until batter sizzles. Cook vegetables first, then meat skimming off cooked batter. Cook until golden. Drain on paper towels and serve immediately.

Combine soy sauce and Chinese mustard for dipping sauce.

SHAO MAI

This wonderful appetizer provides a great opportunity to make use of the imitation crab and shrimp on the market and you can't tell the difference from the fresh.

1 lb imitation crab or shrimp
(or fresh, if available)
1/4 lb mushrooms, chopped finely
1 cup bean sprouts, chopped
3 scallions, thinly sliced
1/2 lb ground pork
2 large garlic cloves, minced
2 tablespoons soy sauce
3 tablespoons dry sherry
1 teaspoon sesame oil (optional)
1 package round wonton wrappers

Soy sauce
Chinese mustard

Lightly brown ground pork and garlic; drain completely. Add mushrooms, bean sprouts, scallions, soy sauce, sherry and sesame oil and mix thoroughly. Place one heaping teaspoon full of mixture in the center of a wonton wrapper and bring the sides up to resemble a bag. Continue until filling is used. Lightly oil a steamer basket and place Shao Mai in a single layer. Cover and cook over boiling water for 20 minutes. (Do not let water touch the bottom of Shao Mai). Mix soy sauce and mustard to desired taste (the mustard is hot) and use as a dipping sauce.

Tropical Cheesecake

Cheesecake is one of the most popular desserts around the world and Hawaii's abundance of fruits make it a refreshing end to any meal. This can be made a day ahead, adding the fruit just before serving.

4 (3 oz) packages Philadelphia
Cream Cheese, room temperature
2 large eggs
1 teaspoon vanilla
1/2 cup sugar
dash cinnamon (optional)
1 pint sour cream
5 tablespoons sugar
Graham cracker crust, 9"
3 oz macadamia nuts, ground
Apple jelly

Beat cream cheese with eggs using an electric mixer or whisk until smooth. Add vanilla, cinnamon and 1/2 cup sugar and beat. Cover graham cracker crust with macadamia nuts and top with cream cheese mixture. Bake at 325° for 25 minutes until set. Cool. Add 5 tablespoons sugar to sour cream and pour on pie. Bake at 325° for 20 minutes until set. Cool. Just before serving, top cheesecake with your choice of sliced or whole fruit in a decorative pattern. Melt apple jelly and brush over fruit. (Note: If you are using bananas, brush with lemon juice to prevent discoloration).